HOW TO BE Y

EMBRACING YOU

Discover How Great You Are
No Matter What Happens

Mahima Bass

Table of Contents

PART 1

Chapter 1:

How Will You Choose To Live Your Life?

How will you choose to live your life? This is something that only you have the power to decide.

We all want different things. As individuals, we are all unique and we have our own ideas about what it means to live a meaningful life. Some treasure family, friends, and relationships above all else, while others prioritise money, material things, careers, and productivity. There is no right or wrong to pursue or place any of these things on a pedestal. If your dream is to build a multi-billion dollar company, then go ahead and chase that dream. If you prioritise just being as stress-free as possible, to do as little work as you can, well you can choose to structure your life in such a way as well. As long as it works for you and that you are happy doing so, I would say go for it.

Sure, your priorities might change as you get older and wiser. Embrace that change. We are not always met to move in a linear fashion in life. We should learn to live like water, being fluid, ever-changing, ever-growing, ever-evolving. Our interests, priorities, passions, all change as we move from one stage of life to the next.

Some only realise that they might want to focus on relationships at a certain point in their lives, some might only want to start a family when they reach a certain age. The point is that we never truly know when is the time when we might feel ready to do something, as much as well tell ourselves that we will know.

The best thing we can do for ourselves right now, in this very moment, is to do what we think is best for us right now, and then to make tweaks and adjustments along the way as we travel down that road faithfully.

Trying to plan and control every aspects of our lives rarely ever works out how we imagined it. You see, life will give us lemons, but it can also give us durians. We might get thrown off the road through unexpected changes. Things that challenge our beliefs and our priorities. Health issues, family tragedies, financial meltdowns, natural disasters, these are things that we can never plan for. We may either choose to come out of these things with a clearer plan for our next phase of life, or we may choose to give up and not try anymore.

All of us have the power to choose how we want to live our lives in this very moment. The worst thing you can do right now is not know what your priorities are and to just cruise through life without having at least a short-term vision on what you want to get out of it.

Take the time to reflect every single day to work on that goal, however scary or simple it may be. Never take your eye off the post and just keep traveling down that path until you reach a fork in the road.

Chapter 2:

How To Have The Best Day Everyday

We all have the power to create the kind of day we want to experience every time we go to sleep and wake up the next day.

It is normal to think that we will only have an amazing day when something good happens to us. We believe that good things only happen out of luck, chance, fate, or whatever, but we never think that we can create a good day just by our sheer desire to.

What the best day means to each of us may be different, some prioritise professional accomplishments as their measurement of a great day, some prioritise spending time with as many friends as possibly in a 24 hour period as one that is great. But when we depend on these circumstances, we are never really in full control of our day because bad things can always happen without a rhyme or reason. Our presentation that we have been working months on could suddenly be marred by a technical difficulty, or our friends could cancel on us last minute due to whatever reason.

What we thought would be our best day could turn out to be one filled with disappointments and maybe even loneliness.

I struggle with this all the time. Everytime i had built up the perfect day in my head, something always seem to go wrong somehow and I am left searching for a filler to cover that void. Through the fault of nobody but life getting the way, as it always does, I found out that if I always depended on others to give me the best day, that it rarely ever happens. Occasionally things work out great when I least expect it, but those occurrences are still out of my control.

It is only when we decide for ourselves that we can have the best day regardless of life inserting itself in, that we can truly enjoy every waking moment of our lives. By constantly reminding ourselves that we are grateful to be alive, to live each moment in the present, and to live as though tomorrow might never come, we can truly appreciate the little things in life that we often overlook. We have the best day because we believe that it is.

From the moment that we get out of bed, we appreciate the first breath we take, the first shower that we take, the first meal that we take, and all the little things that make up our wonderful day. Appreciating the fact that we are living with a roof over our heads, that we have clean water to drink, air conditioning to keep us cool, heaters to keep us warm, literally anything and everything around us, there is something to be grateful for.

When we start to notice that our life is truly amazing, we will never have to depend on other things or other people to make us have our best day. That is the kind of control we have over our day if we set it off on the right foot from the get-go.

It was only when I started being grateful for the fact that I am truly blessed with an amazing family, pet, friends, a house, that I realized i didn't need fancy party or fancy things to allow me to have the best day ever. Yes there are moments in life when we feel truly alive, those moments we will cherish and remember, but those moments are also few and far between. If we can take control of the other 364 days of the year, we would truly be the happiest people alive on this earth who are living their best days everyday.

Chapter 3:

Happy People Consciously Nurture A Growth Mindset

"Without continual growth and progress, such words as improvement, achievement, and success have no meaning." – Benjamin Franklin

Learning is perceived and generally acknowledged by those of us who have gone through primary and university tutoring. We were routinely encircled by people who energized and upheld our developments. Groundbreaking thoughts and change were anticipated from us; the sky was the limit!! However, shouldn't something be said about once we got into the work environment? For some, we subsided into the everyday daily practice, getting it done, uninformed of the cost that our agreeable, monotonous, continuous tasks appeared to have on our own and expert development.

Do you hear employees saying, "I don't get how this venture's development works" or "I'm awful at giving introductions. If it's not too much trouble, let another person do it." If this is the case, reconsideration of your group's growth mindset might be in order. They are working under a "fixed mentality." According to an examination concentrate via Carol Dweck of Stanford University, a fixed attitude happens when individuals accept fixed qualities that can't change. These individuals archive abilities instead of attempting to foster them. On the other hand, a development attitude accepts that knowledge can develop with time and experience. When individuals accept they can add to their learning, they understand exertion affects their prosperity.

You can attempt to battle a fixed attitude and energize a sound growth mindset by rehearsing the following:

Recognize fixed mindset patterns

To begin with, would you say you are ready to precisely recognize and uncover the negative quirks coming about because of a fixed mentality? Normal practices of these individuals incorporate the individuals who keep away from challenges, surrender effectively, consider there to be as achieving nothing, overlook and keep away from negative criticism, need heading in their objectives, and carry on when feeling undermined by other people who make progress. These are normal signs that employees are battling to see their part in supporting the new turn of events.

Energize feedback over praise

Commendation feels better. We like to feel approved in our qualities and are content to let it be the point at which we get acclaim over achieved work—employees to request input despite the result. There are consistent approaches to improve and create. Lead your group to request tips and innovative manners by which they can move toward new situations.

Pinpoint skills and limitations

Take time out from the ordinary daily schedule to pinpoint your workers' qualities and shortcomings will give an unmistakable beginning stage to an initiative in realizing where holes exist. Have workers independently take strength evaluations and meet with them to go over outcomes. Some may feel compromised and cautious while going over shortcomings, yet having a direct discussion on the finding will prompt better anticipation and recuperating.

Chapter 4:

How Distraction Robs You of Joy

How many of you crave the satisfaction that distraction brings you? Whether it be checking your phone regularly for messages, or scrolling through social media apps such as Facebook, instagram, or even mindlessly browsing through streaming apps such as youtube or netflix in search of some form of content that can take your attention away from the work that is actually in front of you that you should be working on?

I believe that many of us crave these distractions because of a few key reasons. Let us see if any of these sound familiar to you, and after I've identified them i will tell you why distraction is actually not the answer to your problems.

The first reason is that we are probably bored and we want to fill that boredom with stuff just so that we can keep ourselves busy and to pass time. I would raise my hand and say that I am guilty of that.

The second reason is that we are probably subconsciously unhappy with what we are doing, whether it be our jobs, or our careers, we feel that we are not doing what we are meant to do and it is causing us anxiety, fear, and worry, and we turn to distractions as a form of therapy to try and calm our nerves, or just temporarily forget our problems for just enough time to feel good before we begin our work again. Does that sound like you?

The third reason is that we are just so engrossed in the new world of information consumption that we have become so addicted to our smartphones or smart appliances, that we willingly give 1/3 of our day away to be mindlessly consuming content that is not beneficial to our lives on this earth. The abundance of apps, streaming platforms, and mobile games, have given us a portal into another dimension away from the physical world. This distracts us from the important stuff we need to do every day to better our lives such as building meaningful relationships with friends, spending time with loved ones, and being present in whatever you are doing.

So why is distraction so harmful that it robs us of real joy and happiness?

From a physiological standpoint, distraction actually uses up a lot of our cognitive capacity to switch from a tasks which requires deep focus. When you are very productive, your brain is actually in a flow state of mind where productivity becomes much easier to achieve. You have undivided attention to complete the task at hand and your brain is working to the best of its ability to provide you with the information that you need to solve whatever problems the job requires. But when you receive a text or decide to take a quick break to check your phone and to scroll through social media, you are actually snapped out of that flow state of mind. And your mind goes into a passive state. And as you revert back to the task you were originally doing, not even mentioning the inertia and the amount of energy it takes to restart your work, your brain actually has to go through the painful process of connecting those cells from your working memory once again. costing you immense amounts of resources and energy. And as you do this probably tens of times each hour, you lose more and more of that focus and eventually you feel tired and unproductive.

And as you spiral downwards, your level of satisfaction drops and so does your sense of joy because you feel unaccomplished, you've wasted hours of time, and you may even start beating yourself up for such a poor performance.

So what action steps can you do to free yourself from distraction so that you can regain control of your energy and time?

Well the very first step, which is probably the simplest but harder to do, is to put your phone on silent mode, or keep it somewhere out of sight so that you are not tempted to reach for it. Turn off all possible forms of distraction that can jeopardise your workflow. And refrain from taking breaks as much as you can, even going to the toilet. Every minute you step away from what you are doing will cost you some form of energy in one way or another. You can even download the app "forest" which actually locks your phone down for a duration you have set for yourself, while at the same time planting a beautiful tree in your garden. It is quite rewarding to see that you have grown a tree after spending a full hour working. And as you feel more productive, your level of happiness will increase from the sense of accomplishment you feel that you got your work done in record time.

The next thing you can do is to start re-assessing the work you are doing. Ask yourself if you are truly happy at your job, because maybe u use distraction as an escape which could indicate that you are probably not doing what you were meant to do. If you really loved your job, you will be in a state of mind where your job doesn't even feel like job anymore and you just want to keep working because you are passionate about it. If that means changing your careers or trying something new, don't be afraid to do so.

The final step is to constantly remind yourself of the value of time and that time is not infinite. We only have so many hours in a day, do we really want to spend half of it on things on mindless content that does not improve ourselves as a person? Time is precious and we should spend it as wisely as we can, free of distraction, and doing meaningful work to better someone else's lives. And as we do these things, we can slowly start to regain control, which helps us become more self-disciplined. And this loop reinforces the good principles we should follow to achieve success and happiness.

Chapter 5:
Happy People Choose to Exercise

There is a feeling you get when you just finish your workout, and you feel amazing, much better than you were feeling before. Even when you are not feeling motivated to go to the gym, just thinking about this feeling makes you get up, leave your bed and get going to the gym. This feeling can also be called an endorphin rush. Exercise indeed makes you happier in multiple ways.

Firstly, movement helps you bond with others that are in the brain chemistry of it all. Your heart rate is going up, you are using your body, engaging your muscles, your brain chemistry will change, and it will make it easier for you to connect and bond with other people. It also changes how your trust people. Research also showed that social pressures like a hug, laughing, or high-five are also enhanced. You will also find your new fitness fam, the people you will be working out with, and because you will have a shared interest that is having a healthy lifestyle will help you have a stronger bond with them. And as experts say that having strong relationships and connections in life will help you in overall happiness.

We have already discussed those exercise increases endorphins but what you do not know is that it increases a lot more brain chemicals that make you feel happy and good about yourself. Some of the brain chemicals that increase are; dopamine, endorphins, endocannabinoid and adrenaline. All of these chemicals are associated with feeling confident, capable, and happy. The amount of stress, physical pain, and anxiety also decrease significantly. A chemical that your body creates when your muscles contract is called "myokine", it is also shown to boost happiness and relieve stress.

Secondly, exercise can help boost your confidence, and of course, when it comes to feeling empowered and happy, confidence is the key. "At the point when you move with others, it's anything but a solid feeling of 'greater than self' probability that causes individuals to feel more idealistic and enabled, "Also, it permits individuals to feel more engaged turning around the difficulties in their own lives. What's more, that is a fascinating side advantage of moving with others because there's an encapsulated feeling of 'we're in the same boat' that converts into self-assurance and the capacity to take on difficulties in your day; to day existence."

Thirdly, exercising outdoors affects your brain, similar to meditation. In case you're similar to the innumerable other people who have found out about the advantages of contemplation yet can't make the time, uplifting news. You may not need to contemplate to get a portion of the advantages. Researchers found that exercising outside can similarly affect the cerebrum and disposition as reflection. Exercising outside immediately affects a state of mind that is amazingly incredible for wretchedness and nervousness. Since it's anything but a state in your mind that is the same as contemplation, the condition of open mindfulness,"

Chapter 6:

Hitting Rock Bottom

Today we're going to talk about a topic that I hope none of you will have to experience at any point in your lives. It can be a devastating and painful experience and I don't wish it on my worst enemy, but if this happens to be you, I hope that in today's video I can help you get out of the depths and into the light again.

First of all, I'm not going to waste any more time but just tell you that hitting rock bottom could be your blessing in disguise. You see when we hit rock bottom, the only reason that we know we are there is because we have become aware and have admitted to ourselves that there is no way lower that we can go. That we know deep in our hearts that things just cannot get any worse than this. And that revelation can be enlightening. Enlightening in the sense that by simple law of physics, the worse that can happen moving forward is either you move sideways, or up. When you have nothing more left to lose, you can be free to try and do everything in your power to get back up again.

For a lot of us who have led pretty comfortable lives, sometimes it feels like we are living in a bubble. We end up drifting through life on the comforts of our merits that we fail to stop learning and growing as people. We become so jaded about everything that life becomes bland. We stop trying to be better, we stop trying to care, and we that in itself could be poison. It is like a frog getting boiled gradually, we don't notice it until it is too late and we are cooked. We are in fact slowly dying and fading into irrelevance.

But when you are at rock bottom, you become painfully aware of everything. Painfully aware of maybe your failed relationships, the things you did and maybe the people you hurt that have led you to this point. You become aware that you need to change yourself first, that everything starts with growing and learning again from scratch, like a baby learning how to walk again. And that could be a very rewarding time in your life when you become virtually fearless to try and do anything in your power to get back on your feet again.

Of course all this has to come from you. That you have to make the decision that things will never stay the same again. That you will learn from your mistakes and do the right things. When you've hit rock bottom, you can slowly begin the climb one step at a time.

Start by defining the first and most important thing that you cannot live without in life. If family means the most to you, reach out to them. Find comfort and shelter in them and see if they are able to provide you with any sort of assistance while you work on your life again. I always believe that if family is the most important thing, and that people you call family will be there with you till the very end. If family is not available to you, make it a priority to start growing a family. Family doesn't mean you have to have blood relations. Family is whoever you can rely on in your darkest times. Family is people who will accept you and love you for who you are inspite of your shortcomings. Family is people that will help nurture and get you back on your own two feet again. If you don't have family, go get one.

If hitting rock bottom to you means that you feel lost in life, in your career and finance, that you maybe lost your businesses and are dealing with the aftermath, maybe your first priority is to simply find a simple part time job that can occupy your time and keep you sustained while you figure out what to do next. Sometimes all we need is a little break to clear our heads and to start afresh again. Nothing ever stays the same. Things will get better. But don't fall into the trap of ruminating on your losses as it can be very destructive on your mental health. The past has already happened and you cannot take it back. Take stock of the reasons and don't make the same mistakes again in your career and you will be absolutely fine.

If you feel like you've hit rock bottom because of a failed marriage or relationship, whether it be something you did or your partner did, I know this can be incredibly painful and it feels like you've spent all your time with someone with nothing to show for it but wasted time and energy, but know that things like that happen and that it is perfectly normal. Humans are flawed and we all make mistakes. So yes it is okay to morn over the loss of the relationship and feel like you can't sink any lower, but don't lose faith as you will find someone again.

If hitting rock bottom is the result of you being ostracised by people around you for not being a good person, where you maybe have lost all the relationships in your life because of something you did, I'm sure you know the first step to do is to accept that you need to change. Don't look to someone else to blame but look inwards instead. Find time where you can go away on your way to reflect on what went wrong. Start going through the things that people were unhappy with you about and start looking for ways to improve yourself. If you need help, I am here for you. If not, maybe you might want to seek some professional help as well to dig a little deeper and to help guide you along a better path.

Hitting rock bottom is not a fun thing, and I don't want to claim that I know every nuance and feeling of what it means to get there, but I did feel like that once when my business failed on me and I made the decision that I could only go up from here. I started to pour all my time and energy into proving to myself that I will succeed no matter what and that I will not sit idly by and feel sorry for myself. It was a quite a journey but I came out of it stronger than before and realized that I was more resourceful than I originally thought.

So I challenge each and everyone of you who feels like you've hit the bottom to not be afraid of taking action once again. To be fearless and just take that next right step forward no matter what. And I hope to see you on the top of the mountain in time to come.

I hope you've learned something today. Take care and I'll see you in the next one.

Chapter 7:

How To Worry Less

How many of you worry about little things that affect the way you go about your day? That when you're out with your friends having a good time or just carrying out your daily activities, when out of nowhere a sudden burst of sadness enters your heart and mind and immediately you start to think about the worries and troubles you are facing. It is like you're fighting to stay positive and just enjoy your day but your mind just won't let you. It becomes a tug of war or a battle to see who wins?

How many of you also lose sleep because your mind starts racing at bedtime and you're flooded with sad feelings of uncertainty, despair, worthlessness or other negative emotions that when you wake up, that feeling of dread immediately overwhelms you and you just feel like life is too difficult and you just dont want to get out of bed.

Well If you have felt those things or are feeling those things right now, I want to tell you you're not alone. Because I too struggle with those feelings or emotions on a regular basis.

At the time of writing this, I was faced with many uncertainties in life. My business had just ran into some problems, my stocks weren't doing well, I had lost money, my bank account was telling me I wasn't good enough, but most importantly, i had lost confidence. I had lost the ability to face each day with confidence that things will get better. I felt that i was worthless and that bad things will always happen to me. I kept seeing the negative side of things and it took a great deal of emotional toll on me. It wasn't like i chose to think and feel these things, but they just came into my mind whenever they liked. It was like a parasite feeding off my negative energy and thriving on it, and weakening me at the same time.

Now your struggles may be different. You may have a totally different set of circumstances and struggles that you're facing, but the underlying issue is the same. We all go through times of despair, worry, frustration, and uncertainty. And it's totally normal and we shouldn't feel ashamed of it but to accept that it is a part of life and part of our reality.

But there are things we can do to minimise these worries and to shift to a healthier thought pattern that increases our ability to fight off these negative emotions.

I want to give you 5 actionable steps that you can take to worry less and be happier. And these steps are interlinked that can be carried out in fluid succession for the greatest benefit to you. But of course you can choose whichever ones speaks the most to you and it is more important that you are able to practice any one of these steps consistently rather than doing all 5 of them haphazardly. But I want to make sure I give you all the tools so that you can make the best decisions for yourself.

Try this with me right now as I go through these 5 steps and experience the benefit for yourself instead of waiting until something bad happens.

The very first step is simple. Just breathe. When a terrible feeling of sadness rushes into your body out of nowhere, take that as a cue to close your eyes, stop whatever you are doing, and take 5 deep breathes through your nose. Breathing into your chest and diaphragm. Deep breathing has the physiological benefit of calming your nerves and releasing tension in the body and it is a quick way to block out your negative thoughts. Pause the video if you need to do practice your deep breathing before we move on.

And as you deep breathe, begin the second step. Which is to practice gratefulness. Be grateful for what you already have instead of what you think u need to have to be happy. You could be grateful for your dog, your family, your friends, and whatever means the most to you. And if you cannot think of anything to be grateful for, just be grateful that you are even alive and walking on this earth today because that is special and amazing in its own right.

Next is to practice love and kindness to yourself. You are too special and too important to be so cruel to yourself. You deserve to be loved and you owe it to yourself to be kind and forgiving. Life is tough as it is, don't make it harder. If you don't believe in yourself, I believe in you and I believe in your worthiness as a person that you have a lot left to give.

The fourth step is to Live Everyday as if it were your last. Ask yourself, will you still want to spend your time worrying about things out of your control if it was your last day on earth? Will you be able to forgive yourself if you spent 23 out of the last 24 hours of your life worrying? Or will you choose to make the most out of the day by doing things that are meaningful and to practice love to your family, friends, and yourself?

Finally, I just want you to believe in yourself and Have hope that whatever actions you are taking now will bear fruition in the future. That they will not be in vain. That at the end of the day, you have done everything to the very best of your ability and you will have no regrets and you have left no stone unturned.

How do you feel now? Do you feel that it has helped at least a little or even a lot in shaping how you view things now? That you can shift your perspective and focus on the positives instead of the worries?

If it has worked for you today, I want to challenge you to consistently practice as many of these 5 steps throughout your daily lives every single day. When you feel a deep sadness coming over you, come back to this video if you need guidance, or practice these steps if you remember them on your own.

I wish you only good things and I hope that I have helped you that much more today. Thank you for your supporting me and this channel and if you find that I can do more for you, do subscribe to my channel and I'll see you in the next one. Take care.

Chapter 8:

First Impressions Matter

Today we're going to talk about a simple topic that I hope will help each and every one of you make a good first impression in every meeting you may encounter in the future.

So why bother with making a good first impression in the first place? The answer is fairly simple - people decide very quickly in the first few minutes whether they think you are someone they might want to associate themselves with or not. They see how you look, how you dress, how you carry yourself, and they decide usually fairly quickly about what label they want to tag on you. Humans are judgemental and superficial creatures by nature. Barring all other aspects of your personality, how you look is the first thing that others can deduce about you.

We have all done this at some point in our lives - we make sweeping remarks about the first "hot guy" or "hot girl" that we see, and we we remark at the way they dress and the choices that they make stylistically. We may find ourself immediately attracted to them based on just their looks.

Of course how we carry ourselves is equally important as well. When we go for interviews, when we meet new clients, the vibes that we let out matters. How others perceive us in that first meeting will set the tone on whether we may be asked back for a second interview, or if our clients will continue to decide on whether to work with us moving forward. Sure if we don't do well in the first impression we may have a chance to redeem ourselves in the second chance we get, but I'm sure that's not where you want to end up if given the choice.

So how can we do our best to make a good first impression in any situation?

I want to start by making sure that you know who your audience is. Do your homework and try your best to anticipate what the opposing party might aspect of you. If you are going for a job interview and you know it will be a formal one, do your best to look smart and dress accordingly. Don't show up with your shirts untucked and un-ironed. Ensure that you look the part of the job you are gunning for. Sure things may go wrong during the interview, but at least you showed up looking like you really are serious about the job and that you want to look presentable for your future boss.

If you know that you are going on a first date for example, make a good first impression by also grooming yourself accordingly to attract your partner. I know it may sound incredibly superficial, but if you look into nature, almost all creatures have a way of attracting their mates. Whether it be through colourful feathers in a peacock, or dance rituals in some exotic birds, or a flowing mane of a lion, all these are ways to catch the attention of their potential partners. When someone dresses nicely it shows that they are making an effort to look good and that they are in the business of winning you over.

Now that I've given you some examples of how looking the part can give you a huge boost in your first impressions rating, I want to move on to the next part which is how you actually carry yourself through the things that you say and the actions that you take.

Everyone knows that a pretty face can only carry you so far if you don't have a good personality to match. Sure we may lust for something that looks good on the outside, but if we take a bite from it and it tastes absolutely gastly, I'm sure most of us would eventually run for the hills afterward. The same goes when you go for interviews as well.

The simplest advice I can give for all of you is to be yourself. Don't try to be something that you are not. In most situations, I believe that staying true to who you are and being congruent in what you say is very important. Yes you have to be professional and do your best to showcase your talents in your area of expertise, but beyond that we do need to try our best to be as authentic as possible. Depending on what our motives are and what we want to get out of the first impression meeting, we have to be really clear about our intentions. If our goal is to deceive, you may find it easy to lie our way through the first meeting, but the truth eventually catches up with us when the opposite party finds that we are not up for job or up to the standards that we have set for ourselves in the first session. If we had stayed true to ourselves from the very beginning, our words will hold more credit and questions to our integrity will be kept to a minimal.

If we want to attract a spouse that is kind-hearted and good-willed, it is only natural for us to expect the same if the opposing party gave us the impression that they are. If it was done out of deceit, over time it will slowly creep up as their authenticity stays to crack and we are revealed their true nature. If we expect others to act and behave the way that is congruent with what they show us in the first impression, we should also do the same for others.

Yes I know that I may be going off a tangent of creating good first impressions. But I am also not going to advocate here that we change ourself completely to make a good impression the first time around only to show up like totally different versions of ourselves the next. I always believe that staying true to who you are is the best way to not only make a good first impression, but also to make a lasting and permanent impression. We want to build a strong reputation for ourselves as individuals who are confident and competent at the same time. We want to earn others' trust not out of deceit but out of skill.

If we find ourselves lacking in certain areas, I propose that we work on it on a consistent and daily basis. If we find that maybe we're not happy with the way we look, make a commitment to get to the gym 5 times a week and to eat healthier. If we find ourselves lacking in key soft skills, we may want to take up a course or go for trainings that help us be better in these areas. If we find ourselves lacking in certain skill sets required for particular job that we want, we may want to consider getting further education so that we are qualified in those areas. The bottom line is, we should never stop working on ourselves. Only then can we truly make a powerful first impression that is credible and lasting.

So I challenge each and everyone of you today to make it a point to put making a good genuine first impression at the top of our list for every new person that we meet. Whatever the reason may be, dress up accordingly and present ourselves well so that we may hopefully get the thing that we want.

I hope you learned something today. Take care and I'll see you in the next one.

Chapter 9:

Setting Too High Expectations

Today we're going to talk about the topic of setting too high expectations. Expectations about everything from work, to income, to colleagues, friends, partners, children, family. Hopefully by the end of this video I will be able to help you take things down a notch in some areas so that you don't always get disappointed when things don't turn out the way you expect it to.

Let's go one by one in each of these areas and hopefully we can address the points that you are actively engaged in at the moment.

Let's begin with work and career. Many of us have high expectations for how we want our work life to be. How we expect our companies and colleagues to behave and the culture that we are subjected to everyday. More often that not though, companies are in the business of profit-making and cutting costs. And our high expectations may not meet reality and we might end up getting let down. What I would recommend here is that we not set these expectations of our colleagues and bosses, but rather we should focus on how we can best navigate through this obstacle course that is put in front of us. We may want to focus instead on how we can handle ourselves and our workload. If however we find that we just can't shake off this expectations that we want from working in a company, maybe we want to look elsewhere to companies that have a work culture that suits our personality. Maybe one that is more vibrant and encourages freedom of expression.

Another area that we should address is setting high expectations of our partners and children. Remember that we are all human, and that every person is their own person. Your expectations of them may not be their expectations of themselves. When you impose such an ideal on them, it may be hard for them to live up to. Sure you should expect your partner to be there for you and for your children to behave a certain way. But beyond that everyone has their own personalities and their own thoughts and ideas. And what they want may not be in line with what we want for them. Many a times for Asian parents, we expect our kids to get good grades, get into good colleges, and maybe becoming a doctor or lawyer one day. But how many of us actually understand what our kids really want? How many of us actually listen to what our kids expect of themselves? Maybe they really want to be great at music, or a sport, or even finance. Who's to say what's actually right? We should learn to trust others and let go of some of our own expectations of them and let them become whoever they want to be.

The next area I want to talk about is simply setting too high expectations of yourself. Many times we have an ideal of who we want to be - how we want to look, how we want our bodies to look, and how we want our bank statement to look, amongst many others. The danger here is when we set unrealistic expectations as to when we expect these things to happen. Remember most things in life takes time to happen. The sooner you realise that you need more time to get there, the easier it will be on yourself. When we set unrealistic timelines, while it may seem ideal to rush through the process to get results fast, more often than not we are left disappointed when we don't hit them. We then get discouraged and may even feel like a failure or give up the whole process entirely. Wouldn't it be better if we could give ourselves more time for nature to work its magic? Assuming you follow the steps that you have laid out and the action plans you need to take, just stretch this timeline out a little farther to give yourself more breathing room. If you feel you are not progressing as fast as you had hoped, it is okay to seek help and to tweak your plans as they go along. Don't ever let your high expectations discourage you and always have faith and trust in the process even when it seems hard.

One final thing I want to talk about is how we can shift from setting too high expectations to one of setting far-out goals instead. There is a difference. Set goals that serve to motivate you and inspire you to do things rather than ones that are out of fear. When we say we expect something, we immediately set ourselves up for disappoint.

However if we tell ourselves that we really want something, or that we want to achieve something that is of great importance to us, we shift to a goal-oriented mindset. One that is a lot healthier. We no longer fear the deadline creeping up on us. We instead continually work on getting there no matter how long it takes. That we tell ourselves we will get there no matter what, no matter how long. The key is to keep at it consistently and never give up.

Having the desire to work at an Apple store as a retail specialist, I never let myself say that I expect apple to hire me by a certain time otherwise I am never pursuing the job ever again. Rather I tell myself that being an Apple specialist is my dream job and that I will keep applying and trying and constantly trying to improve myself until Apple has no choice but to hire me one day. A deadline no longer bothers me anymore. While I wait for them to take me in, I will continue to pursue other areas of interest that will also move my life forward rather than letting circumstances dictate my actions. I know that I am always in control of my own ship and that I will get whatever I put my mind to eventually if I try hard enough.

So with that I challenge each and every one of you to be nicer to yourselves. Lower your lofty expectations and focus on the journey instead of the deadline. Learn to appreciate the little things around you and not let your ego get in the way.

I hope you learned something today, take care and I'll see you in the next one.

Chapter 10:

Figuring Out Your Dreams

Today we're going to talk about dreams and why it is important that we all have some form of a dream or aspiration that we can work towards.

For many of us who are educated in the traditional school system, we process from one grade to the next without much thought and planning besides getting into a good school. And this autopilot has caused many kids, including myself, to not have a vision of my future and what I would like to become when I grow up. We are all taught in some shape or form that we would need to choose a career and pursue that path. Dedicating years of higher education and hundreds of hours of curriculum work only to find ourselves hating the course that we had spent all this time and energy undertaking when we step into our jobs.

This has caused many to start doubting and questioning what we ought to really do with our lives and we might get really anxious because this was certainly not part of the plan that we had set out since we were young.

What I have found personally is that I spent the time and effort to pursue a higher education not because I really wanted To, but rather to appease my parents that they did not waste all their time and money on producing me with proper schooling.

I did not however, go into my field of practice that I had spent the prior 3 years studying for. Instead upon graduating, that was when I really started to figure out what I really wanted to do with my life. Luckily for my parents, they were willing to give me the time and space to explore different possible passions and to carve out a path on my own.

I realised that as I started exploring more, and learning more about myself, the dream that I thought i once had started to change. Instead of dreaming of the perfect job and having the perfect boss, I now dreamt of freedom. To achieve freedom of time to pursue my passions, and to take steps that would move me one step closer to that dream as soon as possible.

Why this particular dream you ask? As i started exploring on successful people who have made it big in life, I realized that those that were truly happy with what they were doing, were not doing things for the money, but rather that they were able to quit their full time jobs to pursue their interests because somehow they had found a way to achieve time freedom that is irrespective of money. It amazed me how many found success by having the freedom to work from home, to not be bound by a desk job or to be hounded on my their bosses. Some live for the climb up the corporate ladder, but i knew that wasn't going to work for me. And I knew i had to make something else work to survive.

So i decided to dedicate my time and energy to only doing things that would help me achieve freedom and that became my dream to retire early and live off my past works.

The takeaway for today is that I want you to give yourself the chance to explore different things and take a step back to assess whether your current dream will actually serve you well in the long run, or if u don't even have a dream, whether you need to take time off to go find that dream for yourself.

I challenge each and everyone of you today to keep an open mind that dreams can change and you can always pursue a new path should you choose to. Because as the saying goes, the only constant in life is change.

Take care and I'll see you in the next one.

PART 2

Chapter 1:

How Getting Out of Your Comfort Zone Could Be The Best Thing Ever

A comfort zone is best described as the place where you feel comfortable and your abilities are not being tested, or a place where you don't have to try anything new or different. We have all heard the advice of getting out of our comfort zone. Its sure sounds like an easy phrase, but any advice is easier to give than to take. While it is true that the ability to take risks by stepping outside your comfort zone is the primary way by which we grow, it's also true that we are often afraid to take that first step. Embracing new experiences can bloom your life and could even change the direction of your career. Comfort zones are not really about comfort; and they are about fear. So, break the chains and step out; you will enjoy the process of taking risks and growing. Here are some ways to get out of your comfort zone to experience a better life.

1. Become Aware Of What's Outside The Comfort Zone

You believe so many things are worth doing, but the thought of disappointment and failure always holds you back. Identify the things that you are afraid of doing and assess the discomforts associated with them. Start working on them slowly and gradually. You will see how much progress you will make and how much you will grow following that. Once your discomforts no longer scare you, you will see how confident you will become in trying new things.

2. Have A Clear Sight About What You Have To Overcome

There would be many situations that get you anxious and uncomfortable. Please make a list of all of them and go deeper. The primary emotion associated with all of our negative thoughts that we try to overcome is fear. Are you afraid of public speaking because you are insecure about your voice? Do you get nervous around people and avoid talking to them for fear of being ignored? Be specific in your areas of discomfort, and then work on your insecurities to get more confident.

3. Get Comfortable With Discomfort

Expand your comfort zone to get out of it. Make it your goal to stop running away from the discomforts. If you can't make eye contact while talking, try locking it a bit more rather than immediately looking out. If you stay long enough and practice it, it will start to become less uncomfortable.

4. See Failure As A Teacher

Many of us are so scared of failures that we would prioritize doing absolutely nothing other than taking a shot at our dreams and goals. We have to treat our failures as a teacher. We learn more from failures than we do from successes. Take that experience that has caused you to fail and evaluate how you can take that lesson your next time so that the chance of success increases. Many of the world's famous people, and even billionaires and millionaires, failed the thousandth time before succeeding.

5. Take Baby Steps

Don't try to achieve everything at once. If you jump outside your comfort zone, the chances are that you will become overwhelmed and jump right back in. Always start by taking small steps, overcome the fear of little things first. It's the small steps along the journey that ensures our extraordinary destination. If you are afraid of public speaking, start by speaking to a smaller group of people or even your family and friends. This will help you built self-confidence, and you will be ready to talk on public platforms in no time.

6. Hang out with risk-takers:

If you want to become better at something, start hanging out with people who already took the risk, who already are doing the things you planned to do. Start emulating them. No one can give you the best insight into the situations than those who already have experienced it. Almost inevitably, their influence will start affecting your behavior, and you too will get a clear mind about things.

7. Be Honest With Yourself

Stop making excuses for the things that you are too afraid to do. You might be tricking your brain into thinking that maybe you don't have enough time to do your tasks. But in reality, you are scared of giving it a chance and risking failure. Don't make excuses but instead, be honest. You will be in a better place to confront what is truly bothering you, and this will increase your chance of moving forward.

8. Identify New Opportunities

Staying in your comfort zone is like sitting in a closed room or wearing blinders. You will convince yourself that you already dislike the things you didn't even try yet and only care about the already part of your life. But you have to put your walls down, not thickens them, and take risks. You will be amazed at how many opportunities you will be exposed to when you finally let yourself out.

Conclusion

It will seem scary at first to get out of your comfort zone, but it will be the best experience of your life. Don't jump right out of it; slowly push yourself past your comfort zone. You will eventually feel more and more comfortable about the new stuff you were too afraid to try.

Chapter 2:

Doing The Thing You Love Most

Today we are going to talk about following your heart and just going for your passion, even if it ends up being a hobby project.

Many of us have passions that we want to pursue. Whether it be a sport, a fitness goal, a career goal, or simply just doing something we know we are good at. Something that electrifies our soul. Something that really doesn't require much persuasion for us to just go do it on a whim.

Many of us dare not pursue this passion because people have told us time and time again that it will not lead to anywhere. Or maybe it is that voice inside your head that is telling you you should just stick to the practical things in life. Whatever the reasons may be, that itch always seem to pester us, calling out to us, even though we have tried our best to put it aside.

We know what our talents are, and the longer we don't put it out there in the world, the longer we keep it bottled up inside of us, the longer the we will regret it. Personally, Music has always been something that has been calling out to me since i was 15. I've always dabbled in and out of it, but never took it seriously. I found myself 14 years later, wondering how much i could've achieved in the music space if i had just leaned in to it just a little.

I decided that I had just about put it off for long enough and decided to pursue music part time. I just knew deep down inside me that if i did not at least try, that i was going to regret it at some point again in the future. It is true that passions come and go. We may jump from passion to passion over the course of our lives, and that is okay. But if that thing has been there calling out to you for years or even decades, maybe you should pay closer attention to it just a little more.

Make your passion a project. Make it a hobby. Pursue it in one form or another. We may never be able to make full careers out of our passions, but we can at least incorporate it into our daily lives like a habit. You may find ourselves happier and more fulfilled should you tap that creative space in you that has always been there.

Sure life still takes precedence. Feeding the family, earning that income, taking care of that child. But never for one second think that you should sacrifice doing what truly makes you happy for all of that other stuff, no matter how important. Even as a hobby, pursuing it maybe 30mins a day, or even just an hour a week. It is a start and it is definitely better than nothing.

At the end of the day passions are there to feed our soul. To provide it will some zest and life to our otherwise mundane lives. The next time you hear that voice again, lean in to it. Don't put it off any longer.

Chapter 3:

Why You're Demotivated By Lack of Clarity

Clarity is key to achieving any lasting happiness or success.
Demotivation is almost certain without clarity.

Always have a clear vision of what you want and why you want it.
Every detail should be crystal clear as if it were real.
Because it is.
Mustn't reality first be built on a solid foundation of imagination.
Your skills in visualisation and imagination must be strong to build that foundation.

You must build it in the mind and focus on it daily.
You must believe in it with all your heart and your head will follow.
Create it in the mind and let your body build it in reality.
That is the process of creation.

You cannot create anything in reality without clarity in the mind.
Even to make a cup of coffee, you must first imagine making a cup of coffee.
It doesn't take as much clarity as creating an international company,
but focus and clarity are required nonetheless.

The big goals often take years of consistent focus, clarity and commitment.
That is why so few succeed.

Demotivation is a symptom of lack of direction.
To have direction you must have clarity.

Embracing You

To have clarity you must have a clearly defined vision of you future.

Once you have this vision, never accept anything less.
Clarity and vision will begin your journey,
but your arrival depends on stubbornness and persistence.

Before you start you must decide to never quit, no matter what happens.
Clarity of your why will decide this for you.
Is the pain you are about to endure stronger than your reasons?

If you are currently demoralised by lack of clarity,
sit down and decide what will really make you happy.
Once you have decided, begin to make it feel real with pictures around your house.
Listen to motivational music and speeches daily to build your belief in you.

Visit where you dream you will be one day.
Get a feel for your desired new life.
Create actions that will build clarity in your vision.
Let it help you adjust to your new and future reality.

Slowly adjust your vision upwards.
Never adjust downwards.
Never settle for less.

The more real your vision feels the more likely it will be.
Begin to visualise living it.
Before long you will be living it.

Adopt the mannerisms of someone who would be in that position.
When you begin to believe you are important, others will follow.
Carry yourself like a champion.
Soon you will be one.

Have clarity you have about who you are.

Have clarity about what you are going to do.

Motivate yourself to success.

Once you step on that path you will not want to return to the you of yesterday.

You will be committed to becoming even better tomorrow.

You will be committed to being the new person you've always known you could be.

Always strive to get another step closer to your vision.

Work until that vision becomes clearer each day.

Have faith that each week more opportunities for progression will present themselves to you.

Clarity is the key to your success.

Chapter 4:

Meditate For Focus

Meditation calms the mind and helps you to focus on what is important. It dims the noise and brings your goals into clearer vision.

Meditation has been practised as far back as 5000bc in India - with meditation depicted in wall artisan from that period.
That is 1500 years older than any written artefact ever found.
It is as old as the archaeological evidence of any human society.

Meditation can change the structure of the brain promoting focus, learning and better memory, as well as lowering stress and reducing the chances of anxiety and depression.

Whilst there are many different types and ways to meditate,
the ultimate goal is to clear your mind and calm your body
so that you can focus on your dream.
Aim to look inward for answers.
It could be aided by music relating to your dream or videos.
The music, the images, and imagining you are already living that life will bring it into reality.

Your mind creates the vision and the feeling
in your heart will bring it to you.
When your mind and heart work together it creates balance,
leading to happiness and success.

Meditation is the process of bringing the
visions of the mind and the desires of the heart together,
which in turn will form your life.
Meditation clears all the threats to this -
such as worry and distraction.
It will bring you clear focus and open up the next steps in your journey.

Meditation is often best done when you first wake or before you go to
sleep, but it can be incorporated into your day.
If clear consistent thought brings decisive action and success,
it is important to dwell on your dreams as often as possible.
Calm your mind of the unnecessary noise that is robbing you of your
focus.

The more realistic you make this vision
and the more you feel it in your heart,
the quicker it will come.

Meditation can help you achieve this
whether you follow a guide or make it up yourself.
The key is calm and focus.

Your subconscious knows how to get there.
Meditation will help open up that knowledge.

Science is just beginning to unlock the answers on why meditation is so effective, even so it has been used for over 7000 years to help people relax and focus on their goals.

The positive health and well-being evidence of meditation is well documented.

We may not yet understand it fully,

But just know that it works and use it every day.

You don't need to understand every detail to use something that works.

Meditation is perhaps one of the most time tested tools in existence.

It could work for you, if you try it.

It could change your life forever.

Chapter 5:

5 Tips to Increase Your Attention Span

If you've ever found it difficult to get through a challenging task at work, studied for an important exam, or spent time on a finicky project, you might have wished you could increase your ability to concentrate.

Concentration refers to the mental effort you direct toward whatever you're working on or learning at the moment. It's sometimes confused with attention span, but attention span refers to the length of time you can concentrate on something.

If that sounds familiar, keep reading to learn more about research-backed methods to help improve your attention span. We'll also go over some conditions that can affect concentration and steps to take if trying to increase concentration on your own just doesn't seem to help.

1. Train Your Brain

Playing certain types of games can help you get better at concentrating. Try:

- sudoku

- crossword puzzles

- chess

- jigsaw puzzles

- word searches or scrambles

- memory games

Results of a 2015 study Trusted Source of 4,715 adults suggest spending 15 minutes a day, five days a week, on brain training activities can greatly impact concentration.

Brain training games can also help you develop your working and short-term memory, as well as your processing and problem-solving skills.

Older adults

The effects of brain training games may be particularly important for older adults since memory and concentration often tend to decline with age.

Research from 2014Trusted Source that looked at 2,832 older adults followed up on participants after ten years. Older adults who completed between 10 and 14 cognitive training sessions saw improved cognition, memory, and processing skills.

After ten years, most study participants reported they could complete daily activities at least as well as they could at the beginning of the trial, if not better.

2. Get Your Game On

Brain games may not be the only type of game that can help improve concentration. Newer research also suggests playing video games could help boost concentration.

A 2018 study looking at 29 people found evidence to suggest an hour of gaming could help improve visual selective attention (VSA). VSA refers to your ability to concentrate on a specific task while ignoring distractions around you.

Its small size limited this study, so these findings aren't conclusive. The study also didn't determine how long this increase in VSA lasted.

Study authors recommend future research continue exploring how video games can help increase brain activity and boost concentration.

3. Improve Sleep

Sleep deprivation can easily disrupt concentration, not to mention other cognitive functions, such as memory and attention.

Occasional sleep deprivation may not cause too many problems for you. But regularly failing to get a good night's sleep can affect your mood and performance at work.

Being too tired can even slow down your reflexes and affect your ability to drive or do other daily tasks.

A demanding schedule, health issues, and other factors sometimes make it difficult to get enough sleep. But it's important to try and get as close to the recommended amount as possible on most nights.

Many experts recommend adults aim for 7 to 8 hours of sleep each night.

4. Make Time For Exercise

Increased concentration is among the many benefits of regular exercise. Exercise benefits everyone. A 2018 study looking at 116 fifth-graders found evidence to suggest daily physical activity could help improve both concentration and attention after just four weeks.

Another Source looking at older adults suggests that just a year of moderate aerobic physical activity can help stop or reverse memory loss that occurs with brain atrophy related to age.

Do what you can

Although aerobic exercise is recommended, doing what you can is better than doing nothing at all. Depending on your fitness and weight goals, you may want to exercise more or less.

But sometimes, it just isn't possible to get the recommended amount of exercise, especially if you live with physical or mental health challenges.

5. Spend Time In Nature

If you want to boost your concentration naturally, try to get outside every day, even for just 15 to 20 minutes. You might take a short walk through a park. Sitting in your garden or backyard can also help. Any natural environment has benefits.

Scientific evidence increasingly supports the positive impact of natural environments. Research from 2014Trusted Source found evidence to suggest including plants in office spaces helped increase concentration and productivity and workplace satisfaction, and air quality.

Try adding a plant or two to your workspace or home for a range of positive benefits. Succulents make great choices for low-maintenance plants if you don't have a green thumb.

Chapter 6:

Overcoming Tiredness and

Lethargy

Tiredness and lethargy has become a major problem for youths and adults these days. As our lives get busier and our ability to control our sleep gets more out of hand, we all face a constant struggle to stay alert and engaged in our life's work every single day. And this problem hits me as well.

You see, many of us have bad sleep habits, and while it might feel good to stay up late every night to watch Netflix and binge on YouTube and Instagram posts, we pay for it the next day by being a few hours short of a restful night when our alarm wakes us up abruptly every morning.

We tell ourselves that not needing so much sleep is fine for us, but our body tells us a different story. And we can only fake being energetic and awake for so long. Sooner or later we will no doubt experience the inability to function on an optimal level and our productivity and mood will also be affected accordingly. And this would also lead to overall tiredness and lethargy in the long run.

Before we talk about what we can do to counter and fix this problem that we have created for ourselves, we first have to understand why we consciously allow ourselves to become this tired in the first place.

I believe that many of us choose entertainment over sleep every night is because we are in some ways or another overworked to the point that we don't have enough time to ourselves every single day that we choose to sacrifice our sleep time in order to gain back that few hours of quality personal time. After spending a good 10 hours at our jobs from 9-6pm, and after settling down from the commute home and factoring in dinner time, we find ourselves with only a solid 1-2 hours of time to watch our favourite Netflix shows or YouTube, which i believe is not very much time for the average person.

When presented with the choice of sleep versus another episode or two of our guilty pleasure, it becomes painfully obvious which is the "better" choice for us. And we either knowingly or unknowingly choose entertainment and distraction over health.

Basically, I believe the amount of sleep you choose to give yourself is directly proportionate to how happy you are about your job. Because if you can't wait to get up each and everyday to begin your life's work, you will give yourself the best possible sleep you can each night to make sure you are all fired up the next day to crush your work. But conversely, if you hate your job and you feel like you have wasted all your time at work all day, you will ultimately feel that you will need to claim that time back at night to keep yourself sane and to keep yourself in the job no matter how much you dislike it. Even if it means sacrificing precious sleep to get there.

So I believe the real question is not how can we force ourselves to sleep earlier every night to get the 8 hours of sleep that we need in order not to feel tired and lethargic, but rather is there anything we can change about how we view our job and work that we come home at the end of the day feeling recharged and fulfilled to the extend that we don't have to look for a way to escape every night into the world of entertainment just to fill our hearts.

When you have found something you love to do each day, you will have no trouble going to bed at 10pm each night instead of 1 or 2am.

So I challenge each and everyone of you to take a hard look at WHY you are not getting enough sleep. There is a high chance that it could boil down to the reason I have described here today, and maybe a change in careers might be something to consider. But if you believe that this tiredness and lethargy is born out of something medical and genetic, then please do go see a doctor to get a medical solution to it.

Otherwise, take care and I wish you all the best in reclaiming back your energy to perform at your peak levels of success. See you in the next one.

Chapter 7:

Constraints Make You Better: Why the Right Limitations Boost Performance

It is not uncommon to complain about the constraints in your life. Some people say that they have little time, money, and resources, or their network is limited. Yes, some of these things can hold us back, but there is a positive side to all of this. These constraints are what forces us to make choices and cultivate talents that can otherwise go undeveloped. Constraints are what drives creativity and foster skill development. In many ways reaching the next level of performance is simply a matter of choosing the right constraints.

How to Choose the Right Constraints

There are three primary steps that you can follow when you are using constraints to improve your skills.

1. **Decide what specific skill you want to develop.**

The more specific you are in the skill, the easier it will be to design a good constraint for yourself. You shouldn't try to develop the skill of being "good at marketing," for example. It's too broad. Instead, focus on learning how to write compelling headlines or analyze website data— something specific and tangible.

2. Design a constraint that requires this specific skill to be used

There are three main options for designing a constraint: time, resources, and environment.

- **Time:** Give yourself less time to accomplish a task or set a schedule that forces you to work on skills more consistently.

- **Resources:** Give yourself fewer resources (or different resources) to do a task.

- **Environment:** According to one study, if you eat on 10-inch plates rather than 12-inch plates, you'll consume 22 percent fewer calories over a year. One simple change in the environment can lead to significant results. In my opinion, environmental constraints are best because they impact your behavior without you realizing it.

3. Play the game

Constraints can accelerate skill development, but they aren't a magic pill. You still need to put in your time. The best plan is useless without repeated action. What matters most is getting your reps in.

The idea is to practice, experiment with different constraints to boost your skills. As for myself, I am working on storytelling skills these days. I have some friends who are amazing storytellers. I've never been great at it, but I'd like to get better. The constraint I've placed on myself is scheduling talks without the use of slides. My last five speaking engagements have used no slides or a few basic images. Without text to rely on, I have designed a constraint that forces me to tell better stories so that I don't embarrass myself in front of the audience.

So, the question here is What do you want to become great at? What skills do you want to develop? Most importantly, what constraints can you place upon yourself to get there? Figure these things out and start from today!

Chapter 8:

Happy People Have A Morning Ritual

For many of us, mornings begin in a rushed panic. We allow our alarm clocks to buzz at least a dozen times before deciding we have to get out of bed. Then we rush around our homes half-awake, trying to get ready for our day. In a hurry, we stub our toe on the bedpost, forget to put on deodorant, and don't pack a lunch because we simply don't have time. It's no wonder that so many folks despise the thought of being awake before 9 a.m.!

So it may not surprise you to know that the happiest and healthiest people tend to enjoy their mornings. They appear to thrive on waking up with the sun and look forward to a new day of possibilities. These people have humble morning rituals that increase their sense of well-being and give their day purpose.

Here are 3 morning habits that healthy and happy people tend to share:

1. They wake up with a sense of gratitude

Practicing gratitude is associated with a sense of overall happiness and a better mood—so it makes sense that the happiest and healthiest people we know start the day with a gratitude practice. This means that they're truly appreciative of their life and all of its little treasures. They practice small acts of gratitude in the morning by expressing thankfulness to their partner each morning before they rise from bed. They may also write about their gratefulness for five minutes each morning in a journal that they keep by their bedside.

2.   They begin every morning anew.

The happiest and healthiest people know that every day is a brand-new day—a chance to start over and do something different. Yesterday may have been a complete failure for them, but today is a new day for success and adventure. Individuals who aren't ruined by one bad day are resilient creatures. Resiliency is a telltale sign of having purpose and happiness.

3.   They take part in affirmation, meditation, or prayer.

Many of the happiest folks alive are spiritual. Affirmations are a way of reminding ourselves of all that we have going for us, and they allow us to engrain in our minds the kind of person we wish to be. Meditation helps keep our mind focused, calms our nerves, and supports inner peace. If you're already spiritual, prayer is a great way to connect and give thanks for whatever higher power you believe in.

Chapter 9:

Discovering Your Purpose

If you guys don't already know, this is one of the topics that I really love talking about. And I never get tired of it. Having a purpose is something that I always believe everyone should have. Having a purpose to live, to breathe, to get up each day, I believe that without purpose, there is no point to life.

So today we're going to talk about how to discover your purpose, and why you should make it a point to find one if you didn't already start looking.

So what is purpose exactly. A purpose is a reason to do something. Is to have something else greater than ourselves to work for. You see, I believe if we are only focused on ourselves, instead of others, we will not be able to be truly happy in life. Feeding our own self interests does not bring us joy as one might think. After living the life that I had, I realized that true happiness only comes when you bring joy to someone else's life. Whether it be helping others professionally or out of selflessness, this happiness will radiate and reflect back to us from someone else who is appreciative of your efforts.

On some level, we can look into ourselves to be happy. For example being grateful for life, loving ourselves, and all that good stuff. Yes keep doing those things. But there is a whole other dimension if we devote our time and energy into helping others once we have already conquered ourselves. If you look at many of the most successful people on the planet, after they have acquired an immense amount of wealth, many of them look to passion projects or even philanthropy where they can give back to the community when having more money doesn't do anything for them anymore. If you look at Elon Musk and Jeff Bezos, these two have a greater purpose which is their space projects. Where they visualise humans being able to move out of Earth one day where civilisation is able to expand. Or Bill Gates and Warren Buffet, who have pledged to give billions of their money away for philanthropic work, to help the less fortunate and to fund organisations that work towards finding cures to diseases.

Now for us mere mortals, we don't need to think so big. Our purpose need not be so extravagant. It can be as simple as having a purpose to provide for your loved one, to work hard to bring your family members of holidays and travel, or to bring joy to your elderly relatives by organising activities for them to do. There is no purpose that is too big or too small.

Your purpose could be helping others find a beautiful home, doing charitable work, or even feeding and providing for your growing family.

As humans, we will automatically work harder if we have a clear and defined purpose. We have a reason to get up each day, to go to work, to earn that paycheck, so that we can spend it on things and people, even ourselves at times. Without a purpose, we struggle to find meaning in the work that we do. We struggle to see the big picture and we find that we have no reason to work so hard, or even at all. And we struggle to find life worth living.

This revelation came to me when I started seeing my work as helping some other person in a meaningful way. Where my work was not just about making money to buy nice things, but to be able to impact someone else's life in a positive way. That became my purpose. To see them learn something new, and to bring a joy and smile to their faces. That thought that I was contributing something useful to someone made me smile more than money ever could. Yes money can help you live a comfortable life, but helping others can go a much farther way into giving your life true purpose.

So I challenge each and everyone of you to find a purpose in everything that you do, and if you struggle to find one, start by making the goal to help others a priority. Think of the difference you can make to others and that could very well be your purpose in life as well.

I believe in each and every one of you.. I hope you learned something today and as always, take care and I'll see you in the next one.

Chapter 10:

Dealing With Addiction To

Technology

Today we're going to talk about addiction to technology and media consumption. I think this is a topic that many of us can relate, even myself included. Am my goal for today is to try to help put forth a more sustainable and healthy habit for you to still enjoy technology while not being overwhelmed and overtaken by it completely.

So lets ask ourselves a simple question of why are we so hooked into using our devices so frequently and sparingly? I think for most of us, and this is my personal opinion, is that it offers us an escape, a distraction from our every day tasks that we know we ought to do. To procrastinate just a little bit or to binge scroll on Instagram, Facebook, Snapchat, and what have you, to satisfy our need for media consumption.

We use technology as a tool a gateway into the world of digital media, and we get lost in it because companies try to feed us with posts and stuff that we like to keep us engaged and to keep us watching just a little while longer. And minutes can turn into hours, and before you know it, it is bedtime.

I want to argue that this addiction is not entirely your fault, but that these multi billion dollar mega companies are being fed so much data that they are able to manipulate us into consume their media. It is like how casinos use various tricks of flickering lights, and free drinks to keep you playing a little longer and to spend a little more of your attention and time. We unknowingly get subjected to these manipulative tactics and we fall for it despite our best efforts to abstain from it.

I for one have been the subject of such manipulation. Whether it be Netflix or my favourite social media apps, I find myself mindlessly scrolling through posts trying to get my quick fix of distraction and supposed stress relief. However these feelings dont bring me joy, rather it brings me anxiety that I have wasted precious time and I end up kicking myself for it afterwards. This happens time and time again and it felt like I was stuck in a loop, unable to get out.

So what is the solution to this seemingly endless spiral of bad habits? Some might say just to delete the apps, or turn off wifi. But how many of you might have actually tried that yourself only to have it backfire on you? Redownloading the app is only one step away, wifi is only one button away, and addictions aren't so easily kicked to the curb as one might think.

What I have found that works is that instead of consuming mindless media that don't bring about actual benefit to my life, I chose to watch content that I could actually learn something from. Like this channel for example. I went on the hunt to seek out content that I could learn how to make extra money, how to improve my health, how to improve my relationships, basically anything that had to do with personal development. And I found that I actually felt less guilty watching or reading these posts even though they still do take up my time to consume.

You may call it a lesser of two evils, but what I discovered was that it provided much more benefit to my life than actually not consuming any personal development media at all. Whether it be inspirational stories from successful entrepreneurs like Elon Musk, or Jeff Bezos, or multi billion dollar investment advice from Warren Buffet, these passive watching of useful content actually boosted my knowledge in areas that I might otherwise have not been exposed to. Subconsciously, i started internalizing some of these beliefs and adopted it into my own psyche. And i transformed what was mindless binge watching of useless Tv shows and zombie content, to something that actually moved the needle in my life in the right direction, even by a little.

Overtime, I actually required less and less distraction of media consumption using my technology devices like iPhones and iPads or Macs, and started putting more attention and effort to do the work that I knew i had to get done. Because some of these personal development videos actually taught me what I needed to do to get stuff done and to stop procrastinating in working towards my goals.

So I challenge each and everyone of you today to do a thorough review of the kinds of music and media consumption that you consume today with your smartphones and tablets, and see if you can substitute them with something that you can learn from, no matter how trivial you think it may be. It could be the very push you need to start porting over all your bad habits of technology into something that can pay off for you 10 years down the road.

I hope you learned something today, and I'll see you in the next one.

PART 3

Chapter 1:

Showing Up

Today we are going to talk about the simple concept of "Showing Up".
And this is going to touch on the topic of motivation as well.

You see for many of us who struggle with laziness and a lack of willpower, we wait for inspiration to strike, or the perfect storm of feeling good and motivated before we make the effort to hit the hit or start taking action on the task that we have been putting off. We think that we need to be all pumped up and excited before doing anything, but many a times, these feelings are few and they rarely come when we expect them to.

There are days where I would plan a gym session only to cancel because I didn't feel like it. And there are times when I would plan a meetup with my friends only to feel lazy at the last second and cancelling. And there are also times when I plan to work at a particular cafe but decided against it because I was too tired.

All these moments where I lacked the willpower to get things started or keeping to my word only made my future commitments even more vulnerable to default. As i was giving in to my desires to be lazy, the next time it came around the excuses became easier and easier to justify. And that only led to a less favourable outcome with regards to my mental, physical, and emotional health. I was spiraling to a life of mediocrity every time i let my inner demon win.

This all changed when I came across an article that said that all you needed to do was to show up for your activity, even if u didn't want to. Just to do a quick 5 min session rather than a long 1 hour session that i would normally have planned out. Or to simply just get to the desk to work for 15mins rather than the 5 hours I would normally have set aside time to do.

I found that by the simple act of showing up for my activity, I had given myself the best possible chance to fulfilling that promise to myself. At the gym, one rep turned into 10 reps, and 5 mins of workout turned into a 2 hour one as i told myself you can do one more, and one more after that. And as I watched people workout around me, i felt motivated to put in more effort in my workout as well. This simple change made it easier for me to simply show up the next day at the gym and let the process play out on its own once again. The same principle came to work and play. I realised that all i needed to do was to get out of the house and the rest would take care of itself. To show up at my desk and gym, no matter how late I may be, that at least when I am there, I will begin the task one way or another.

I challenge each and everyone of you to give it a try. If you find the task that you dread to be too daunting, that Instead of setting a specific time that you need to spend on it, that you simply just show up. And let your body dictate how much time you should indeed spend on that activity. Be it 5 mins or 5 hours. I have found that once I start something that it takes a lot of energy for me to stop. It is like a moving train or car, that once u get going you will most probably go till you can't go no more. Then you slowly grind to a halt and show up for the next activity.

I hope you have learned something today and I wish you all the best in getting your stuff done ASAP. Take care and i'll see you in the next one.

Chapter 2:

Overcoming Your Fears

Today we're going to talk about the topic of fears. What fear is and how we can overcome it. Now before we dive into it, let us just take a brief moment to think of or right down what our greatest fears are right now.

Whether it be taking the next step in your relationship, fear of the unknown, fear of quitting your job and not finding another one, fear or death, fear of illnesses, whatever fear that jumps out at you and is just eating at you at the back of your mind, i want you to remember that fear as we go through this video.

So what is fear exactly? Whilst there are many definitions of fear out there, I'm going to take, as usual, my spin on things. And to me fear is simply a negative feeling that you assign to usually a task that you really don't want to do. And most of the time, the fear is of the unknown, that you can't visualise what is going to happen next. You don't know whether the outcome will be good or bad, and you don't know whether it is the right move to make. So this trio of thoughts keep circling round and round and eventually you just decide that you are not going to take any action on it and you just shove it to one side hoping that it goes away. And whilst you may do that temporarily, sometimes even for months, one day you are going to have to come face to face with it again. And when that day comes, you will either be paralysed again or you may again put it off to a later date.

We procrastinate on our fears because we want a sure thing. We want to know what will happen next, and we fear what we don't know.

Now for the fears that we are talking about today, it is something that will affect your life if u don't take action. If it is like a fear of bungee jumping or sky driving, sure that fear is physical and very real, but also you can make a choice not to do it and your problem is solved. It will not affect your life in a negative way if u don't do it.

But if it is a fear of a career switch because you already hate your job so much and are totally miserable, that is a fear that you should do your best to try and address as soon as possible.

So what can and should you do about these sorts of fears? The answer for this one is not going to be that difficult. Simply think of the consequences of not conquering your task and how much it might prevent you from moving forward in life and you have got your answer.

When the pain associated with not accomplishing the task becomes greater than the fear we assign to it, it is the tipping point that we need to finally take that action. But instead of waiting to get to that excruciating pain, we can visualise and project what it could potentially feel like if we don't do it now and the pain we might feel at a later day, say 1 year from now, when we have wasted another full year of our life not taking that leap of faith, the time we have burned, the time we can never get back, and the opportunity cost of not taking action now, we might just decide that we don;t want to wait until that day comes and face that huge amount of regret that we should've done something a lot sooner.

And what we need to simply do is to just take action. Taking action is something you will hear from all the gurus you will find out there. When faced with a fear or challenge, instead of wondering what dangers lurk in the unknown, just take action and let the experience tell you whether it was indeed the right or wrong decision. Do you necessary homework and due diligence beforehand and take that calculated step forward instead of procrastinating on it. Life is too short to be mucking around. Just go for it and never live your life in fear or regret ever again.

I challenge each and everyone of you to go through the list that we have created at the start of the video. The one that you have been most fearful of doing. And i want you to assess the pros and cons of each fear that you have written down. If there are more pros than cons, i want you to set a deadline for yourself that you will take action on it. And that deadline is today. Don't waste precious time worrying and instead spend more time doing.

I hope you learned something today and as always take care and i wish you all the best in overcoming your fears and achieving your goals as fast as possible. See you in the next one.

Chapter 3:

Planning Ahead

The topic that are going to discuss today is probably one that is probably not going to apply to everybody, especially for those who have already settled down with a house, wife, kids, a stable career, and so on. But i still believe that we can all still learn something from it. And that is to think about planning ahead. Or rather, thinking long term.

You see, for the majority of us, we are trained to see maybe 1 to 2 years ahead in our lives. Being trained to do so in school, we tend to look towards our next grade, one year at a time. And this system has ingrained in us that we find it hard to see what might and could happen 2 or 3 years down the road.

Whilst there is nothing wrong with living life one year at a time, we tend to fall into a short term view of what we can achieve. We tell ourselves we must learn a new instrument within 1 year and be great at it, or we must get this job in one year and become the head of department, or we must find our partner and get married within a short amount of time. However, life does not really work that way, and things actually do take much longer, and we do actually need more time to grow these small little shoots into big trees.

We fail to see that we might have to give ourselves a longer runway time of maybe 3-5 or even 10 years before we can become masters in a new instrument, job, relationship, or even friendships. Rome isn't built in a day and we shouldn't expect to see results if we only allow ourselves 1 year to accomplish those tasks. Giving ourselves only 1 year to achieve the things we want can put unnecessary pressure on ourselves to expect results fast, when in reality no matter how much you think u think rushing can help you achieve results faster, you might end up burning yourself out instead.

For those short term planners, even myself. I have felt that at many stages in my life, i struggle to see the big picture. I struggle to see how much i can achieve in lets say 5 years if i only allowed myself that amount of time to become a master in whatever challenge i decide to take on. Even the greatest athletes take a longer term view to their career. They believe that if they practice hard each day, they might not expect to see results in the first year, but as their efforts compound, by the 5th year they would have already done so much practice that it is statistically impossible not to be good at it.

And when many of us fall into the trap of simply planning short term, our body reacts by trying to rush the process as well. We expect everything to be fast fast fast, and results to be now now now. And we set unrealistic goals that we cannot achieve and we beat ourselves up for it come December 31st.

Instead i believe many of us should plan ahead by giving ourselves a minimum of 2.5 years in whatever task we set to achieve, be it an income goal, a fitness goal, or a relationship goal. 2.5 years is definitely much more manageable and it gives us enough room to breathe so that we don't stress ourselves out unnecessarily. If you feel like being kinder to yourself, you might even give yourselves up to 5 years.

And again the key to achieving success with proper long term planning is Consistency. If you haven't watched my video on consistency do check it out as i believe it is one of the most important videos that I have ever created.

I believe that with a run time of 5 years and consistency in putting the hours every single day, whether it is an hour or 10 hours, that by the end of it, there is no goal that you cannot achieve. And we should play an even longer game of 10 years or so. Because many of the changes we want to make in life should be permanent and sustainable. Not a one off thing.

So I challenge each and everyone of you today to not only plan ahead, but to think ahead of the longevity of the path that you have set for yourself. There is no point rushing through life and missing all the incredible sights along the way. I am sure you will be a much happier person for it.

I hope you learned something today, take care and I'll see you in the next one.

Chapter 4:

If Today Was Your Last Day

If today was your last day, what would you do with your life? Steve Jobs once said that "For the past 33 years, I have looked in trhe mirror every morning and asked myself: **'If today** were the **last day** of my life, would I want to do what I am about to do **today?** ' And whenever the answer has been 'No' for too many **days** in a row, I know I need to change something.".".

Do you agree with that statement? For me I believe that it is true to a certain extent. I argue that not many of us have the luxury of doing what we love to do every single day. As much as we want to work at that dream job or earn that great salary, or whatever that ideal may be, for some of us who have to feed a family or make ends meet, it is just not possible. And we choose to make that sacrifice to work at a job that we may not like, or go through a routine that sometimes might seem a drag. But that's a personal choice that we choose to make and that is okay too.

On the flip side, i do believe that for those who have the luxury and the choice to pursue whatever careers, dreams, hobbies, and interests we want to pursue, that we should go for it and not live life in regret. I have heard of countless friends who work at a job they hate day in and day out, complaining about their life every single day and about how miserable they are, but are too afraid to leave that job in fear of not being able to find something they like or in fear that their dreams would not work out. Not because they couldn't afford to do so, but because they are afraid. This fear keeps them trapped in a never ending cycle of unhappiness and missed opportunities.

Personally, I'm in the camp of doing something you dislike even if u struggle with it if it can provide you with some financial security and pay your bills, whilst at the same time pursuing your dreams part time just to test the waters. You have the comfort of a monthly stream of income while also taking a leap of faith and going after what you really want to do in life. And who knows it could work out some day. In the present moment, I'm actually working on many different interests and hobbies. I do the necessary work that i hate but explore other areas that brings me joy, and that is what keeps be going. I have a passion for singing, songwriting, tennis, and making videos like this that not only educates but also aims to bring joy to others. My full-time job only fulfils my bank account while my interests and work that i do on the side fulfils my heart and soul. And who knows, if any one of these side hobbies turn out into something that I can make some money with, hey it's a win win situation now don't you think?

I challenge each and every one of you to go ahead and take a leap of faith. Time waits for no one and you never know when your last day might be. Koby Bryant died suddenly from a helicopter crash at a young age of 41. But I would argue that because he pursued his dreams at a young age, he has already lived a wonderful and fulfilling life as opposed to someone who is too afraid to do what they want and hasn't lived up to their fullest potential despite living until 90. You have also heard of Chadwick Boseman who was immortalised as a great human being who gave it his all despite fighting colon cancer. He pursued his dreams and I bet that he had no regrets that his life had to end earlier than it should. And to Steve jobs, he gave us Apple, the biggest company in the world by pursuing his dream of changing the world and the way we communicate with one another. Without him we wouldn't have all our favourite beloved apple products that we use today. Without him there might not be amazon, google, Facebook because there wouldn't be apps and there wouldn't be devices that people used to do all these things with.

But most importantly, this is about you. How do you want to live your life, and if today was your last day, what would you do differently and how would this carry on to all other areas of your life. Your relationships with your family, your relationship with your friends, your partner. And do you feel fulfilled as a human being or do you feel empty inside. It is never too late to turn your life around and make choices that will make your heart fill with immense joy and gratitude until your life truly ends. So make the decision right now to honour yourself by living your day to the fullest, coz you never know when it might be your last.

Enjoying The Journey

Today I want to talk about why enjoying the journey of life is important. And why hurrying to get to the destination might not be all that enjoyable as we think it is.

A lot of us plan our lives around an end goal, whether it be getting to a particular position in our company's ladder, or becoming the best player in a sport, or having the most followers on Instagram or whatever the goal may be... Many of us just can't wait to get there. However, many a times, once we reach our goal, whilst we may feel a sense of satisfaction and accomplishment for a brief moment, we inevitably feel like something is missing again and we search for our next objective and target to hit.

I have come to realise that in life, it is not always so much the end goal, but the journey, trials, struggles, and tribulations that make the journey there worth it. If we only focus on the end goal, we may miss out the amazing sights along the way. We will ultimately miss the point of the journey and why we embarked on it in the first place.

Athletes who achieve one major title never stop at just that one, they look for the next milestone they can achieve, but they enjoy the process, they take it one step at a time and at the end of their careers they can look back with joy that they had left no stone unturned. And that they can live their life without regret.

How many times have you seen celebrities winning the biggest prize in their careers, whether it may be the Grammy's Album of the Year if you are a musician, or the Oscars Best Actor or Best Actress Award. How many of them actually feel like that is the end of the journey? They keep creating and keep making movies and film not because they want that award, even though it is certainly a nice distinction to have, but more so because they enjoy their craft and they enjoy the art of producing.

If winning that trophy was the end goal, we would see many artists just end their careers there and then after reaching the summit. However that is not the case. They will try to create something new for as long as people are engaged with their craft, as with the case of Meryl Streep, even at 70+ she is still working her butt off even after she has achieve all the fame and money in the world.

Even for myself, at times i just want to reach the end as quickly as possible. But many times when i get there, i am never satisfied. I feel empty inside and i feel that I should be doing more. And when i rush to the end, i do feel like I missed many important sights along the way that would have made the journey much more rewarding and enjoyable had I told myself to slow it down just a little.

I believe that for all of us, the journey is much more important than the destination. It is through the journey that we grow as a person, it is through the journey that we evolve and take on new ideas, work ethics, knowledge, and many little nuggets that make the trip worth it at the end. If someone were to hand you a grand slam title without having you earned it, it would be an empty trophy with no meaning and emotions behind it. The trophy would not represent the hours of hard work that you have put in to be deserving of that title.

So I challenge each and everyone of you today to take a step back in whatever journey you may be on. To analyse in what aspects can you enjoy the moment and to not place so much pressure into getting to the destination asap. Take it one day at a time and see how the journey you are on is actually a meaningful one that you should treasure each day and not let up.

I hope you enjoyed today's topic and sharing and as always I wish you all the best in your endeavours. I'll see you in the next one.

Chapter 5:

The 5 Second Rule

Today I'm going to share with you a very special rule in life that has worked wonders for me ever since I discovered it. And that is known as the 5 second rule by Mel Robbins.

You see, on a daily basis, I struggle with motivation and getting things done. I struggle with the littlest things like replying an email, to responding to a work request. This struggle has become such a bad habit that before I think about beginning any sort of work, I would first turn on my Netflix account to watch an episode or two of my favourite sitcom, telling myself that I will get right on it after I satisfy this side of me first.

This habit of procrastination soon became so severe that I would actually sit and end up wasting 4-5 hours of time every morning before I would actually even begin on any work-related stuff. Before I knew it, it would be 3pm and I haven't gotten a single thing done. All the while I was staring at the clock, counting the number of hours I have wasted, while simultaneously addicted to procrastinating that I just could not for the life of me get myself off the couch onto my desk to begin any meaningful work.

I realized that something had to change. If I kept this up, I would not only not get anything done, like ever, but i would also begin to loathe myself for being so incredibly unproductive and useless. This process of self-loathing got worse everyday I leaned into the habit of procrastination. It was only until i stumbled onto Mel Robbin's 5 second rule that I started to see a real change in my habits.

The rule is simple, to count backwards from 5 and to just get up and go do that thing. It sounded stupid to me at first, but it worked. Instead of laying around in bed every morning checking my phone before I woke up, I would count backwards from 5 and as soon as it hit 1, i would get up and head straight towards the shower, or I would pack up my things and get out of my house.

I had identified that staying at home was the one factor that made me the most unproductive person on the planet, and that the only way I knew I was going to get real work done, was to get out of the house. I had also identified that showering was a good way to cleanse my mind from the night before. I really enjoyed showering as I always seem to have a clear head afterwards to be able to focus. What works for me, may not necessarily work for you. You have to identify for yourself when are the times you are most productive, and simply replicate it. A good way to find out is by journaling, which I will talk about in a separate video. Journaling is a good way to capture a moment in time and a particular state of mind. Try it for yourself the next time you are incredibly focused, write down how you got to that state, and simply do it again the next time to get there.

The 5 second rule is so simple yet so powerful because it snaps our unhealthy thought patterns. As Mel puts it, our brain is hardwired to protect us. We procrastinate out of fear of doing the things that are hard, so we have to beat our brain to it by disrupting it first. When we decide to move and take action after reaching 1, it is too late for our brains to stop us. And we get the ball rolling.

I was at my most productive on days that I felt my worst. But I overcame it because I didn't let my brain stop me from myself. I wouldn't say that I am struggle free now, but i knew i had a tool that would work most of the time to get me out of procrastination and into doing some serious work that would move my life forward. There are times when I would forget about the 5 second rule and my bad habits would kick in, but I always reminded myself that it was available to me if I chose to use it.

I would urge all of you who are struggling with any form of procrastination or laziness to give the 5 second rule a try. All you need to do is to get started and the rest becomes easy.

Chapter 6:

8 Habits That Can Kill You

Toxic habits in our lives which when left unchecked can lead us to an early grave. We may not be aware of it but it is most definitely eating away at us slowly; like a frog gradually boiling to his death. These invisible yet harmful habits will start appearing in your life if you don't start taking note of it.

Here are 8 habits that can kill you if you're not careful:

1. Being a workaholic.

Man shall eat from the sweat of his brows. Our income pays our bills and puts food on the table. This infers that work is good for it is the backbone on which our survival is pegged upon. It is however not a license to bite more than you can chew. Drowning yourself at work is dangerous for your health.

There is a breaking point for every person. Workaholism is a habit that depressed people do to drown their misery. With only so much that you can handle, you will lose touch with the world if you work without a break. Workaholics are not hard workers who work to make ends meet. They are obsessed with work so that they can forget their problems.

If you are a workaholic who uses business to distract you from your problems, you run the risk of sinking to depression. Take note if stress disorders or suicidal thoughts start to appear. It may be time to seek help to deal with your problems head on instead of masking them in busyness.

2. <u>Isolating yourself from others.</u>

Withdrawal is a red flag any day, anytime. The moment you begin finding comfort in solitude, not wanting to associate with anyone, a problem is in the offing. However, there are times when you will need time alone to meditate and seek peace within yourself.

It is during withdrawal that suicidal thoughts are entertained and sometimes executed. When one isolates themselves from the rest of the world, he becomes blind and deaf to the reality on the ground. You seemingly live in a separate world often mistaken as one of tranquility and peace.

To fight isolation, always find a reason to be around people you share common interests with. It could be sports, writing, acting, or watching. This will help keep off loneliness.

3. <u>Drug and substance abuse.</u>

Drug abuse is a pitfall that many youths have fallen into. It will lead you to an early grave if you do not stop early enough. Apart from the long-term side effects on the health of addicts, drug abuse rips addicts off morality. Most of them become truants, finding themselves on the wrong side of the law and society.

Among the many reasons drug addicts give for drug abuse is that drugs give solace from the harsh world, some kind of temporary blissful haven which the soul longs for. It is unjustifiable to enter into such a health-damaging dungeon to contract respiratory diseases, liver disease, kidney damage, and cardiovascular diseases.

Be careful if you seek drugs as a way to escape from your troubles. If you look closely, most of these people do not end up in a good place after abusing these substances. Seek a healthier alternative instead to let off steam instead.

4. Judging yourself by the standards of others.

As Albert Einstein rightly put it; if we judge a fish by its ability to climb a tree, it will live its whole life believing it is stupid. It is erroneous to use other people's measurement of success to judge your own. This is not to say that you should not be appreciating the achievements of others, but as you do so, give yourself time and space for growth.

The pressure that comes with conforming to your peers' standards can push you down a dark path. Society can be so unforgiving for the faint-hearted. Once you are inside the dark hole of hopelessness, the air of gloom hangs over your head and it can lead you to an early grave. Everyone will forsake you when you fail even after trying to be like them.

5. Being in the wrong company.

Bad company ruins good morals. This truth is as old as civilization. It is not rocket science on how powerful the power of influence from friends is. When in the wrong company, you will be tagged into all sorts of activities they do. Isn't that a direct ticket to hades?

When you lose the power to say No and defend your integrity, morals, and everything that you believe in, then all hell will break loose on you. You would have handed your hypocrite friends the license to ruin your life. Not only will the wrong company ruin your life but also assassinate your character. Keep safe by fleeing from the wrong company when you can before it is too late.

6. Lying.

It looks simple but what many people do not consider is the effect of character assassination caused by a simple lie. Lying makes you unreliable. One client or employer will tell another one and before you know it no one wants anything to do with you.

It may not physically kill you but it will have the power to close all possible open doors of opportunities. Why not be genuine in your dealings and win the trust of your employers and clients? You should jealously protect your reputation because any assault at it is a direct attack on your integrity.

7. Lack of physical exercise.

A healthy body is a healthy mind. To increase your longevity, you need to have a healthy lifestyle. It is not always about the posh vehicle you are driving or the classy estate you live in. How physically fit you are plays a big role in determining your productivity.

You need to walk out there in the sun, go for a morning run, lift weights, do yoga and kegel exercises, or go swimming. Your body needs to be maintained by exercise and not dieting alone. It seems ignoble to be a field person but its benefits are immense.

8. Poor nutritional habits.

The risks of poor nutrition are uncountable. Overeating and obesity come from these habits. Few people pay attention to what they eat, ignorant of the consequences that follow.

Malnutrition and obesity are opposites but stemming from one source – poor nutrition. The eminent danger can no longer be ignored.

According to statistics from the World Health Organization, worldwide obesity has nearly tripled since 1975. In 2016 alone, more than 1.9 billion adults were overweight. The world health body acknowledges that the developmental, economic, social, and medical impacts of the global burden of malnutrition are serious and lasting, for individuals and their families, communities, and countries.

This has come as a shocker to us but it would not have been so if people paid attention to their nutrition habits.

All these 8 habits that can kill you are avoidable if caution is taken. The ball is in your court. Consider carefully whether you want to make a conscious decision to take responsibility and eliminate these damaging habits. You have the power to change if you believe in yourself.

Chapter 7:

6 Ways To Define What Is Important In Your Life

In this crazy world that we live in, the course of evolution spirals upward and downward, and the collective humanity has witnessed glorious times and horrific ones. The events around us change minute-to-minute. So much seems out of our control, but we find solace in knowing that one thing remains within our immediate control; taking back ownership and responsibility for ourselves. If life has gotten away from you and you feel overwhelmed, anxious or depressed, then maybe it's time to stop and refocus on what's most important to you and find a way back to what really matters to you.

The idea is to evaluate what you're actually doing with and for yourself, determine if it's even essential to you, and then make the said necessary changes that will best accommodate your needs, interests, and desires. Here are some ways to consider how and on what things you should refocus your attention to determine what is most important in your life.

1. Determine What Things You Value Most

Choose and focus on the things around which you have to structure the life that you want to create. When you consciously make these choices, you are more focused on reminding yourself what things in your life you can't and won't do without. These all represent the backbone of your life. We often forget that people and events play a massive role in shaping up to our lives. They Mold us into what we have become so far and what we are to become in the future. Their support and encouragement in our lives are undeniable. We have to see which people and what events we value the most in our lives and then should keep our focus on them more.

2. Decide What Commitments Are Essential To You

Keeping the above valuable things in mind, evaluate which commitments do you value the most in your life. Commitments are the obligations you enter into willingly and represent your promise to see any relationship/project/contract conclusion steadfastly. Renegotiate your essential commitments, if necessary, but consider completing the existing commitments that you are already obligated to and refuse to take any new ones if you aren't ready. That way, you will focus more and fulfill those commitments first that are more significant to you and your life.

3. Assess The Way You Use Your Time

Most of us have a fixed daily routine, with many fixed activities, habits, and chores. Evaluate which things are absolutely necessary and vital for shaping up your life and yourself daily. Assess the time you spend communicating, how much of your time you spend online, emailing, texting, or on your cell phone. How can you cut back the amount of time spent on these activities to do something more productive? How much time are you spending on TV, radio, reading newspapers and magazines? Consider decreasing your consumption and receive the basic information from a reputable source only once throughout the day. Avoid repetition and redundancy.

4. Get Rid of Any clutter That's In Your Life

Look around you and see, do you need everything you have? Give away anything that you haven't used since the last two years. It could be anything, from selling items to furniture, clothing, shoes, etc. Anything that you no longer need. Someone else can happily use what you haven't all this time. And not just the worldly things; get rid of all the emotional and psychological clutter you have kept aside for so long, and it no longer serves you. We have to get rid of the old things to make room for the new things to come. This will help us reflect on our actual being of who we are and where we are.

5. Spend More Time With People That Matter To You

Evaluate how much quality time you actually spend with your family and close friends. As life evolves, more people will enter into your sphere. These people may fall into different categories of importance in your life, such as acquaintances, colleagues, friends, partners, etc. Our time is precious, so it is wise to use it on those that matter to us the most. It's necessary to sort out our interactions and to assess the meaning of each relationship to us.

6. Make Time To Be Alone

It all comes down to how much time do you make yourself at the end of the day? What was the last time you spent doing something you're passionate about or what you love doing? Give yourself all the time and permission to express your creativity and make peace with your mind. Take care of your body, spirit, and mind because these are the things that will make you feel alive. Take a walk and look around, reacquaint yourself with all the beauty around you. Make each breath count.

Conclusion

Identifying and understanding your values is a challenging but as well as an essential exercise. Your personal values are a central part of defining who you are and who you want to be. By becoming more aware of these significant factors in your life, you can use them as your best guide in any situation. It's comforting and helpful to rely on your values since most of our life's decisions are based on them.

Chapter 8:

It's Okay To Feel Uncertain

We are surrounded by a world that has endless possibilities. A world where no two incidents can predict the other. A realm where we are a slave to the unpredictable future and its repercussions.

Everyone has things weighing on their mind. Some of us know it and some of us keep carrying these weights unknowingly.

The uncertainty of life is the best gift that you never wanted. But when you come to realize the opportunities that lie at every uneven corner are worth living for.

Life changes fast, sometimes in our favor and sometimes not much. But life always has a way to balance things out. We only need to find the right approach to make things easier for us and the ones around us.

Everyone gets tested once in a while, but we need to find ways to cope with life when things get messy.

The worst thing the uncertainty of life can produce is the fear in your heart. The fear to never know what to expect next. But you can never let fear rule you.

To worry about the future ahead of us is pointless. So change the question from 'What if?' to 'What will I do if.'

If you already have this question popping up in your brain, this means that you are already getting the steam off.

You don't need to fear the uncertain because you can never wreck your life in any such direction from where there is no way back.

The uncertainty of life is always a transformation period to make you realize your true path. These uncertainties make you realize the faults you might have in your approach to things.

You don't need to worry about anything unpredictable and unexpected because not everything is out of your control every time. Things might not happen in a way you anticipated but that doesn't mean you cannot be prepared for it.

There are a lot of things that are in your control and you are well researched and well equipped to go around events. So use your experience to do the damage control.

Let's say you have a pandemic at your hand which you couldn't possibly predict, but that doesn't mean you cannot do anything to work on its effects. You can raise funds for the affected population. You can try to find new ways to minimize unemployment. You can find alternate ways to keep the economy running and so on.

Deal with your emotions as you cannot get carried away with such events being driven by your feelings.

Don't avoid your responsibilities and don't delay anything. You have to fulfill every task expected of you because you were destined to do it. The results are not predetermined on a slate but you can always hope for the best be the best version of yourself no matter how bad things get.

Life provides us with endless possibilities because when nothing is certain, anything is possible. So be your own limit.

Enjoying The Simple Things

Today we're going to talk about a topic that might sound cheesy, but trust me it's worth taking a closer look at. And that is how we should strive to enjoy the simple things in life.

Many of us think we need a jam packed schedule for the week, month, or year, to tell us that we are leading a very productive and purposeful life. We find ways to fill our time with a hundred different activities. Going to this event, that event, never slowing down. And we find ourselves maybe slightly burnt out by the end of it.

We forget that sometimes simplicity is better than complication. Have you sat down with your family for a simple lunch meal lately? You don't have to talk, you just have to be in each other's company and enjoying the food that is being served in front of you.

I found myself appreciating these moments more than I did running around to activities thinking that I needed something big to be worth my time. I found sitting next to my family on the couch watching my own shows while they watch theirs very rewarding. I found eating alone at my favourite restaurant while watching my favourite sitcom to be equally as enjoyable as hanging out with a group of 10 friends. I also found myself richly enjoying a long warm shower every morning and evening. It is the highlights of my day.

My point is that we need to start looking at the small things we can do each day that will bring us joy. Things that are within our control. Things that we know can hardly go wrong. This will provide some stability to gain some pleasure from. The little nuggets in the day that will not be determined by external factors such as the weather, friends bailing on us, or irritating customers.

When we focus on the little things, we make life that much better to live through.

Chapter 9:

6 Ways To Adopt New Actions That Will Be Beneficial To Your Life

There is this myth that goes around saying that, once you leave your teenage, you can never change your Habits. One can analyze this for themselves. Everyone has a list of new year's resolutions and goals. We hope to get these things done to some extent, but, never do we ever really have a clear idea of how to get to those goals in the least possible time.

We always desire a better future but never really know how to bring the necessary change in our lives. The change we need is a change in attitude and behavior towards life altogether. Change is never easy, but it is achievable with some sheer willpower. You might be on the right track to lead a better life, but there are always more and better things to add to your daily habits that can be helpful in your daily life.

Here are 6 simple yet achievable actions you need to take:

1. Decide Today What Is Most Important In Your Life

Life is a constant search for motivation. The motivation to keep doing and changing for the better. Once you have something to change for, take a moment and envision the rest of your life with and without the change you are about to make.

If you have made up your mind, now think about how you can start off with these things. For starters, if you want a healthy lifestyle, start your day with a healthy breakfast and morning exercise on an empty stomach. If you want to scale your business, make a customer-friendly business model.

2. Make Reasonable and Achievable Goals.

Adopting new habits can be challenging, especially if you have to change something in your day-to-day life to get better results. Start easy by making goals that are small, easy, reasonable, and won't give you a headache.

You can start off with baby steps. If you want to become more responsible, mature, and sorted in your life, just start your day by making your own bed, and do your dishes. Ride a bicycle to work, instead of a car or a bus. Things become smooth and easier once you have a reason for the hard acts.

3. Erase Distractions from Your Daily Life

You have wasted a lot already, don't waste any more time. As young as you are right now, you should feel more privileged than the older people around you. You have got the luxury of time over them. You have the right energy and pinnacle moments to seize every opportunity you can grasp.

Don't make your life a cluster of meaningless and profit-less distractions. You don't have to go to every public gathering that you are invited to. Only those that give you something in return. Something that you can avail yourself of in your years to come. Don't divulge in these distractions only for the sake of memories. Memories fade but the time you waste will always have its imprint in every moment that follows.

4. Make a Diary and a Music Playlist

You can devote some time to yourself, just to communicate with your brain and start a discussion with yourself. Most people keep a diary for this purpose, some people tend to make a digital one these days. When you start writing to yourself in the third person, talking and discussing your issues and your weaknesses, you tend to find the solutions within.

Most people find it comforting and calming when they have a playlist of music playing in the background while working. Everyone can try this to check if they get a better level of creativity if they have some small activity that soothes their stressed nerves.

5. Incorporate Regular Walk and Exercise in Your Life

When you know you have a whole day ahead of you, where you have to sit in an office chair for the next 8 hours. Where you have to sit in your home office looking at those sheets for most of the day. A 10 min walk before or after the busy schedule can help a lot in such conditions. You can never avoid physical activities for your whole life, especially if you want to live a healthier and longer life.

People always feel reluctant to exercise and running once they enter college or work life. Especially once they have a family to look out for. But trust me, your body needs that blood rushing once a day for some time. You will feel much more pumped and motivated after a hard 2-mile jog or a 15 min workout.

6. Ask Others for Help and Advice

You have a life to live for yourself, but always remember, you are never too old to ask for help. A human can never perfect something in their life. You will always find someone better than you at a particular task, don't shy to ask for help, and never hold back to ask for any advice.

We feel low many a time in our lives. Sometimes we get some foul thoughts, but we shouldn't ever pounce on them. We should rather seek someone's company for comfort and sharing our concerns.

Conclusion

The ultimate success in life is the comfort you get at the end of every day. Life can never be fruitful, beneficial, and worth living for if we don't arrange our lives as resourceful human beings. Productive minds always find a way to counter things and make the best out of everything, and this is the art of living your life.

Chapter 10:

Distraction Is Robbing You

Every second you spend doing something that is not moving you

towards your goal, you are robbing yourself of precious time.

Stop being distracted!

You have something you need to do,

but for some reason become distracted by

other less important tasks and procrastinate on the important stuff.

Most people do it,

whether it's notification s on your phone or chat with colleges,

mostly less than half the working day is productive.

Distraction can be avoided by having a schedule

which should include some down time to relax

or perhaps get some of them distractions out of the way,

but time limited.

As long as everything has its correct time in

your day you can keep distraction from stealing too much of your time.

When your mind is distracted it becomes nearly impossible to

concentrate on the necessary work at hand.

Always keep this question in mind:

"is what I am about to do moving me towards my goal?"

If not, is it necessary?

What could I do instead that will?

It's all about your 24 hours.

Your actions and the reactions to your actions from that day,

good or bad.

By keeping your mind focused on your schedule that

moves you towards your goal, you will become resilient to distraction.

Distraction is anything that is not on your schedule.

You may need to alter that depending on the importance of the

intrusion.

Being successful means becoming single minded about your goal.

Those with faith do not need a plan b because they know plan A is the

only way and they refuse to accept anything else.

Any time you spend contemplating failure will add to its chances of

happening.

Why not focus on what will happen if you succeed instead?

Distraction from your vision of success is one of its biggest threats.

Blocking out distraction and keeping that vision clear is key.

Put that phone on flight mode and turn off the TV.

Focus on the truly important stuff.

If you don't do it, it will never get done.

The responsibility is all yours for everything in your life.

The responsibility is yours to block out the distractions and exercise your free-will over your thoughts and actions.

By taking responsibility and control you will become empowered.

Refuse to let anyone distract you when you're working.

Have a set time in your schedule to deal with stuff not on the schedule.

This will allow you time to deal with unexpected issues without stopping you doing the original work.

The reality is that we all only have so much time.

Do you really want to waste yours on distractions?

Do you want to not hit your target because of them?

Every time you stop for a notification on your phone you are losing time from your success.

Don't let distraction rob you of another second, minute, hour or day.

Days turn to months and months turn to years don't waste time on distractions and fears.

Saying Yes To Things

Today we're going to talk about why saying yes can be a great thing for you and why you should do so especially in social invites.

Life you see is a funny thing. As humans, we tend to see things one dimensionally. And we tend to think that we have a long life ahead of us. We tend to take things for granted. We think we will have time to really have fun and relax after we have retired and so we should spend all our efforts and energy into building a career right now, prioritising it above all else. When faced with a choice between work and play, sometimes many of us, including myself choose work over social invites.

There were periods in my life that i routinely chose work over events that it became such a habit to say no. Especially as an entrepreneur, the interaction between colleagues or being in social events is almost reduced to zero. It became very easy and comfortable to live in this bubble where my one and only priority in life is to work work work. 24 hours, 7 days a week. Of course, in reality a lot of time was wasted on social media and Netflix, but u know, at least i could sort of pretend that i was kind of working all day. And I was sort of being productive and sort of working towards my goals rather than "wasting time on social events". That was what I told myself anyway.

But life does not work that way. As I prioritised work over all else, soon all the social invite offers started drying up. My constant "nos" were becoming evident to my social circle and I was being listed as perpetually unavailable or uninterested in vesting time or energy into any friendships or relationships. And as i retreated deeper and deeper into this black hole of "working remotely" i found myself completely isolated from new experiences and meeting new people, or even completely stopped being involved in any of my friend's lives.

I've successfully written myself out of life and I found myself all alone in it.

Instead of investing time into any meaningful relationships, I found that my closest friends were my laptop, tablet, phone, and television. Technology became my primary way of interacting with the world. And I felt connected, yet empty. I was always plugged in to wifi, but i lived my life through a screen instead of my own two eyes. My work and bedroom became a shell of a home that I spent almost all my time, and life just became sort of pointless. And I just felt very alone.

As I started to feel more and more like something was missing, I couldn't quite make out what it was that led me to this feeling. I simply though to myself, hey I'm prioritising work and my career, making money is what the internet tells me I should do, and not having a life is simply part of the price you have to pay... so why am I so incredibly unhappy?

As it turns out, as I hope many of you have already figured out at this point, that life isn't really just about becoming successful financially. While buying a house, getting a car, and all that good stuff is definitely something that we should strive towards, we should not do so at the expense of our friends. That instead of saying no to them, we should start saying yes, at least once in a while. We need to signal to our friends that hey, yes even though I'm very busy, but I will make an effort to carve out time for you, so that you know I still value you in my life and that you are still a priority.

We need to show our friends that while Monday may not work for us, that I have an opening maybe 2 weeks later if you're still down. That we are still available to grow this friendship.

I came to a point in my life where I knew something had to change. As I started examining my life and the decisions I had made along the way with regards to my career, I knew that what I did wrong was saying no WAAAAAY too often. As I tried to recall when was the last time I actually when I went out with someone other than my one and only BFF, I simply could not. Of the years that went by, I had either said that I was too busy, or even on the off chances that I actually agreed to some sort of meetup, I had the habit of bailing last minute on lunch and dinner appointments with friends. And I never realized that i had such a terrible reputation of being a flaker until I started doing some serious accounting of my life. I had become someone that I absolutely detested without even realising it. I have had people bail on me at the very last minute before, and I hated that feeling. And whenever someone did that to me, I generally found it difficult to ask them out again because I felt that they weren't really that interested in meeting me anyway. That they didn't even bother to reschedule the appointment. And little did I know, I was becoming that very same person and doing the very thing that I hate to my friends. It is no wonder that I started dropping friends like flies with my terrible actions.

As I came to this revelation, I started panicking. It was as if a truck had hit me so hard that I felt that I was in a terrible accident. That how did I let myself get banged up to that extent?

I started scrolling through my contact lists, trying to find friends that might still want to hang out with me. I realized that my WhatsApp was basically dry as a desert, and my calendar was just work for the last 3 years straight with no meaningful highlights, no social events worth noting.

It was at this point that I knew I had made a huge mistake and I needed to change course immediately. Salvaging friendships and prioritising social activities went to the top of my list.

I started creating a list of friends that I had remotely any connection to in the last 5 years and I started asking them out one by one. Some of my friends who i had asked out may not know this, but at that point in my life, i felt pretty desperate and alone and I hung on to every meeting as if my life depended on it. Whilst I did manage to make some appointments and met up with some of them. I soon realized that the damage had been done. That my friends had clearly moved on without me... they had formed their own friends at work and elsewhere, and I was not at all that important to have anymore. It was too little too late at that point and there was not much I could do about it. While I made multiple attempts to ask people out, I did not receive the same offers from people. It felt clearly like a one-way street and I felt that those people that I used to call friends, didn't really see me as one. You see growing a friendship takes time, sometimes years of consistent meetups before this person becomes indispensable in your life. Sharing unique experiences that allow your friends to see that you are truly vested in them and that you care about them and want to spend time with them. I simply did not give myself that chance to be integrated into someone's life in that same way, I did not invest that time to growing those friendships and I paid the price for it.

But I had to learn all these the hard way first before I can receive all the good that was about to come in the future.

In the next piece, I will show how i actually turned my life around by putting myself in positions where I will be exposed to more chances of social activity. And when saying yes became critical to growing a new social network for myself.

CPSIA information can be obtained
at www.ICGtesting.com
Printed in the USA
BVHW040845271221
624880BV00018B/1071